DK Eye Wonder

Rainforest

Northamptonshire
County Council
Libraries and Information Service

10/1/06	20 MAY 2008	06 FEB 2009
24/1/06		22 FEB 2010
16 JUN 2007		19 MAR 2010
20/01/07		06 DEC 2018
25/02/08		

GREENWOOD, E.

Rainforest

Northampto
DISCARDE
Librarie

Please return or renew this item by the last date shown.
You may renew items (unless they have been requested by another customer) by telephoning, writing to or calling in at any library. 100% recycled paper BKS 1 (5/95)

D1081450

80 002 379 138

A PEARSON COMPANY

Northamptonshire Libraries & Information Service

Peters	01-Jul-04
577.34	£4.99

Written and edited by Elinor Greenwood
Designed by Tory Gordon-Harris

Publishing manager Mary Ling
Managing art editor Rachael Foster
Jacket design Chris Drew
Picture researcher Nicole Kaczynski
Production Kate Oliver
DTP Designer Almudena Díaz
Zoology consultant Helen Sharman

First published in Great Britain in 2001 by
Dorling Kindersley Limited
80 Strand, London WC2R 0RL

2 4 6 8 10 9 7 5 3 1

Copyright © 2001 Dorling Kindersley Limited, London
First paperback edition 2004

A CIP catalogue record for this book
is available from the British Library.

All rights reserved. No part of this publication may be reproduced, stored in a retrieval system, or transmitted in any form or by any means, electronic, mechanical, photocopying, recording, or otherwise, without the prior written permission of the copyright owner.

Paperback edition ISBN 1-4053-0470-7
Hardback edition ISBN 0-7513-3229-1

Colour reproduction by Colourscan, Singapore
Printed and bound in Italy by L.E.G.O.

see our complete
catalogue at
www.dk.com

Contents

4-5
Welcome to the jungle

6-7
Forest layers

8-9
The variety of life

10-11
Giant trees

12-13
Jeepers creepers

14-15
In the treetops

16-17
Flying high

18-19
Tree-houses

20-21
Canopy creatures

22-23
Forest acrobats

24-25
Happy families

26-27
The understorey

28-29
Going batty

30-31
Camouflage

32-33
Lying low

34-35
Insect armies

36-37
Hunting

38-39
Riverbanks

40-41
Watery world

42-43
Night life

44-45
Exploring the jungle

46
Glossary

47
Animal alphabet

48
Index and
acknowledgements

Forest facts

- Tropical rainforests only cover a small area of the world (7%).
- Over half the world's wildlife lives in the rainforests.
- The largest area of tropical rainforest is the Amazon jungle in South America.
- Jungle soil is shallow, only 10 cm (4 in) deep, yet some of the tallest trees in the world grow in it.

Fragile forests

Rainforests help to clean the world's air and water. Jungle plants give us medicines that make us well when we are ill. Rainforests are very important but are shrinking every day – chopped down for land and wood. We need to value these amazing forests, and take care of all the animals that live in them.

Welcome to the jungle

Monkeys call loudly from giant trees, huge spiders scuttle across your feet, and insects as big as dinner plates buzz around your ears. You're in the jungle!

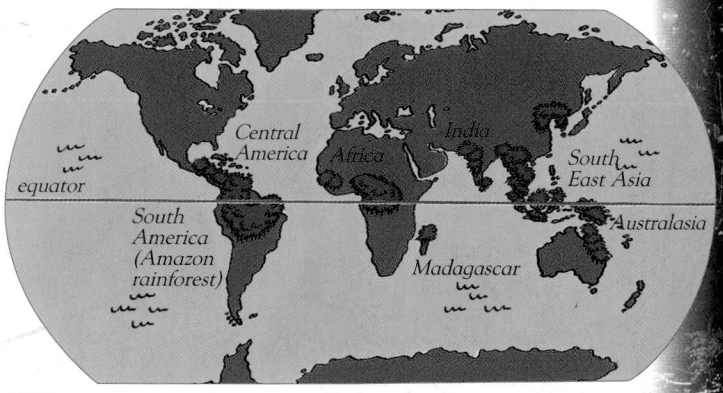

Where in the world...

Tropical rainforests are found either side of the equator – an imaginary line that circles the globe like a belt. The weather near the equator provides perfect conditions for lush forests to grow.

Weather forecast

It's easy to guess the daily weather forecast in the jungle – hot and humid with heavy rain. Some areas of tropical rainforests get a massive 4 m (160 in) of rain each year and the temperature is always between 75 and 80 °F (24-27 °C).

Shades of green

Getting lost in the rainforest can be a real problem. The best way to travel through it is by boat. Many rivers snake through the jungle, carrying excess rainwater towards the sea.

Animal magic

There is an incredible amount of different animals living in tropical rainforests. They are mostly very shy, however, and are experts at doing disappearing acts among the leaves.

Baby gorillas, like this one, live with their families in African jungles.

Forest layers

Each animal has its own special place in the rainforest. They may visit their neighbours, or eat out now and then, but they always return home. From the tips of trees to the forest floor, each layer of the forest has a name. Follow this guide to climbing a jungle tree, starting from the bottom.

Emergent layer

It is much more windy above the canopy. The huge crown of the tree spreads out above you, forming the "emergent" layer. Here tribes of agile monkeys swing through the trees. You're as high as a church steeple so don't look down!

The canopy

The next layer – called the "canopy" – is made up of the thick branches and leaves of taller trees. A refreshing breeze and dappled sunlight make this the most popular place to live in the jungle – more wildlife lives here than anywhere else.

The crown of an emergent tree can spread to be the size of two football pitches.

Storms and high winds lash at the treetops.

Bright green, red, and blue parrots swoop around the treetops.

Emergent trees can be 60 m (200 ft) high.

Forest facts

- The canopy is like a leaky roof – it stops most rain from reaching the forest below.
- No-one knows much about the jungle treetops. They are hard to study because they are so high up.

The understorey

Leafy bushes and the tops of small trees make up the first layer, called the "understorey". It is dark and hot here, like on the forest floor. Tiny frogs hide in the leaves, and sparkly birds hover in front of flowers.

The forest floor

The climb starts at the leafy forest floor. A soft carpet of dead leaves is perfect for insects. Anteaters and other insect-munching creatures live here.

Rivers

It is impossible to travel far in the rainforest without crossing one of the many streams and rivers that slice through it. Watch out for crocodiles and deadly piranha fish as you cross!

The variety of life

There is more variety of wildlife in the world's tropical rainforests than anywhere else on Earth. There is so much, in fact, that scientists believe there is still a lot to find.

Rainbow birds
Birds of every colour flash among the trees. This toucan uses its fantastic beak to crack open the many forest fruits, attract toucan friends, and scare away enemies.

Mammals with moustaches
The rainforests support many amazing mammals too, like this emperor tamarin. Mammals are hairy animals that feed their babies with milk.

Forest layers are one of the reasons there is so much variety – life is piled on top of life.

Teeming with bugs
There are far more creepy crawlies than anything else in the animal kingdom, and nowhere is that more obvious than in the rainforests. On just one jungle tree, scientists found 200 different types of ant – that's more than in many countries.

The postman butterfly is one of 2000 species of butterfly found in the Amazon jungle.

New types of insect are found every day in tropical rainforests.

Woody words

Carnivore A meat eater. Poison arrow frogs eat insects so they are carnivores.

Herbivore A plant eater. Leaf-eating iguanas and nectar-drinking butterflies are herbivores.

Omnivore A meat and plant eater. Toucans and tamarins, for example, eat a mixture of fruit and insects.

Scaly reptiles

Reptiles live at every level of the jungle, from big iguanas like this one, to hissing snakes and clever crocodiles. Reptiles have scales on their skin and lay eggs.

Reptiles are close relatives of the dinosaurs – that's why some of them look so fierce!

Amphibians

Brightly-coloured frogs, like this poison arrow frog, are common in jungle trees. Frogs and toads are amphibians, which means they can live in and out of water.

Giant trees

The giants of the jungle, the emergent trees, stick their huge heads out above the canopy. These trees, that start life as tiny saplings on the forest floor, are often hundreds of years old.

Knee-high saplings need sunlight to grow taller.

Starting out

When an old tree crashes to the ground, it makes a clearing. Saplings now have the sunlight they need to grow. They race towards the light, competing to take the dead tree's place.

Wriggly roots

Huge roots, known as buttress roots, wriggle across the forest floor. They make a steady base for the giant trees. These roots also draw up water and nutrients from the top, most fertile, layer of soil.

Spreading out

Once a young tree has grown past the canopy, it can spread out its branches and enjoy the sunshine. No other giant trees can grow nearby because there is not enough room.

Some of the 60-m (200-ft) high giant trees are up to 1,400 years old.

Piggyback plants

Some canopy branches are like long, thin gardens. They are covered with plants, called epiphytes, growing piggyback on the bark. These plants absorb water from the air, or catch it for themselves, to survive. The epiphytes in this picture are called bromeliads.

Epiphytes can be so heavy that an old tree can't bear the weight and falls over.

Bromeliads catch water like buckets. Animals like this tree frog collect around the mini-ponds.

Dead leaves mix with water to make a soupy mulch for the plant to take up.

The roots of bromeliads are only for gripping on. They do not steal nutrients from the tree.

Woody words

Sapling A very young tree.

Nutrients The "food" dissolved in water that helps plants grow healthily.

Fertile Rich in nutrients. Plants and trees grow more quickly and strongly in fertile soil.

Jeepers creepers

Creeper streamers hang between trees and bright red flowers dot the greenery like party decorations. From orchids to rafflesia, rainforests are home to over half the world's plant life.

Lobster claws

On a walk through the Amazon jungle, you are likely to see one of the 450 species of heliconia, also known as lobster claws. These striking flowers love the tropical heat and damp conditions of jungle life.

Orchids

Delicate and exotic orchids perch high on the branches of tall trees. These epiphytes (see page 11) need to be able to absorb water very quickly in order to survive.

Can you spot the orchid mantis in the flower? It is lying in wait to catch visiting insects.

A stinking giant

A 1-m (3-ft) wide rafflesia bloom – the biggest flower in the world – opens in the dead of night and lasts for only one week. It stinks of rotting meat, earning it the nickname "corpse flower".

Thick woody creepers called lianas stretch between trees.

A deadly trap

Insects have a fatal attraction to the sweet nectar in pitcher plants. When they land on the rim, they lose their footing, fall inside, and drown in the fluid at the bottom. The plant then absorbs nutrients from their dead bodies.

Rafflesia have no leaves or greenery. They are parasites, draining all the nourishment and support they need from a host vine.

Where does rubber come from?

Pencil rubbers, bike tyres, and bouncing balls come from rubber trees that were originally found in the Amazon jungle. Two hundred years ago, Europeans flocked to the Amazon to make their fortunes from rubber. Despite it being illegal, they smuggled some trees out to South East Asia. Today, most rubber comes from there.

In the treetops

The animals of the emergent layer make their homes at the very top of the forest. They need a remarkable sense of balance as well as a good head for heights – it's a long way down!

Mighty morphos

Aeroplane pilots flying above the Amazon often notice the blue, shimmering wings of morpho butterflies below them. Morphos are very fast and agile flyers – easy to see, but hard to catch.

Big ears

This common marmoset (a type of monkey) is the size of a squirrel. It is small enough to dart among the trees, catching insects, frogs, and lizards.

Colugo cradle

When it's time to move on, this baby colugo scrambles out of its mother's cradling arms and onto her back. Mum then uses the flaps on her sides to make skin-wings to glide down to lower trees.

Sky diver

The colobus monkey performs spectacular leaps between trees. Its feathery tail helps to steer its jumps as well as slow it down in the air. It will fearlessly dive down 9 m (30 ft) – the height of a two-storey house – to a lower tree.

Colobus monkeys rarely, if ever, go down to the ground.

Roosting roos

Tree kangaroos, the "monkeys" of Australasia (there are no wild monkeys in this area of the world), can leap easily between trees. They have sharp, curved claws on their feet to help them climb.

All kangaroos have babies called joeys. A mother carries her joey in a pouch on her tummy.

Because treetop branches are thin, many animals living here are small and light.

The hairs at the end of its tail spread out mid-leap, like a mini-parachute.

Forest facts

- Jungle animals do move between layers, and may travel down (or up) to find food.
- Animals living in the treetops have to put up with a lot of rain and storms.
- Many amazing birds also enjoy the view from the treetops.

Flying nutcrackers
Macaws, like the ones flying in this flock, have powerful beaks to break open nuts. To them, biting into a nut is as easy as biting into a banana. They are very brightly-coloured birds, and the largest of all the parrots.

Flying high

There are many different types of birds living in the emergent layer, from majestic eagles and vultures, to noisy gangs of colourful parrots.

Parakeets, along with lorikeets and macaws, are a type of parrot.

Screeching parakeets

It's hard to see this parakeet when it's feeding on fruit or flowers amongst the leaves. You can't miss it calling to its friends, though.

Rainbow colours

A very fast bird, this rainbow lorikeet will fly a long way to find food. They usually travel in chattering flocks of 15-20 birds, but sometimes flocks join up and hundreds fly together.

Philippine eagles grow to 1 m (3 ft) tall, and 8 kg (17 lb) in weight – they're definitely not as light as a feather!

Jungle cleaner

King vultures help keep the jungle clean by eating dead animals. They find rotting bodies by following other vultures or using their strong sense of smell.

King vultures have bald heads for delving into carcasses.

One fifth of all the birds in the world live in tropical rainforests.

Monkey eater

This rare Philippine eagle is one of the world's biggest eagles. It has broad, rounded wings to help it swoop among the branches of trees and pick off unlucky monkeys.

Tree-houses

It's bedtime in the forest. Whether it's a daytime nap or a full night's sleep, every animal needs a safe and comfortable place to rest. Many bed down in the trees.

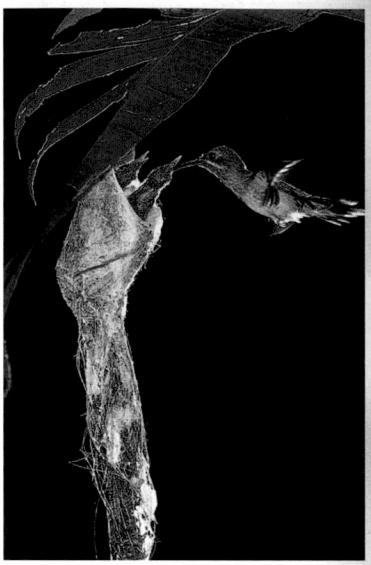

Soft as silk

Hermit hummingbirds are too small and delicate to make their nests out of twigs. Instead they gather spider silk with their beaks and weave it into a silken cup for their tiny chicks.

Spider silk is sticky, so the bird can attach her nest to a leaf. She adds a few twigs to the bottom so that it doesn't blow away.

Palaces for ants

The interconnecting chambers of ant plants make ideal living rooms for countless ants. They use the chambers like a palace, with rooms for nurseries, larders, supplies – and even a special bedroom for the queen.

The plant benefits, too, by gaining nutrients from the debris collected and stored by the ants.

Sweet dreams

Tree frogs, tasty snacks for many predators, like to rest inside snug bromeliads. The thick leaves protect and hide them.

Tree frogs also save on water loss by sleeping through the hotter daylight hours.

A nest of leaves

Orang-utans learn at a young age how to make sleeping nests in the trees. They copy their parents, action for action, until they can build their nests in just a few minutes. They bend back branches to make their bed and then settle down comfortably for the night.

Orang-utans are the largest tree-living animals in the world.

This lucky colugo has found a suitable hole high up in the emergent layer.

Hole owners

There can be fierce competition for tree holes in the rainforest. Many animals and birds, that can't make the holes themselves, prefer to raise their families in the comfort and safety of a tree hole.

A sloth's coat is full of caterpillars that feed on green algae growing in its hair.

Hanging out

Sloths spend their lives hanging upside down. They have strong, hooked claws at the ends of their fingers, like coat hangers (because of these, they can't stand or walk). They move around the trees very slowly. Once a week they climb down to the forest floor to go to the toilet. It takes them about an hour to get there.

This snake gently wraps its coils around sleeping prey...

...and then tightens its grip.

Canopy creatures

More wildlife lives amongst the thick leaves and winding branches of the canopy than anywhere else in the rainforest. Monkeys chatter, reptiles flourish, and strange creatures cling to overhanging branches.

Like their namesakes, squirrel monkeys are very agile and speed through the canopy.

Cheeky monkeys

These fun-loving common squirrel monkeys like to live in big groups of 30 or more friends and family. They eat fruit, birds' eggs, and wouldn't say "no" to a nice, juicy spider, either.

Gentle giant

A green iguana looks fierce but it is really very timid. Even though it can be as long as a man, it will run away at the smallest fright. Iguanas are good climbers, with powerful toes and sharp claws for holding onto branches.

Iguanas store fat under their jaws and in their necks.

One long muscle

A green tree python has a nasty way of killing its prey. It uses its muscular body to squeeze it to death. By day, it drapes itself elegantly on a branch. By night, it hunts for sleeping monkeys and birds.

These bulges are strong mouth muscles for holding onto prey.

Forest facts

- Canopy leaves can be 4 m (13 ft) long – like huge, green umbrellas.
- Epiphytes (see page 11) growing on a canopy branch can weigh as much as the branch.
- Canopy plants flower at different times. Some plants flower six times a year, others only once in 40 years.

Forest acrobats

Whether they are swingers, jumpers, or gliders, animals travel around the treetops with acrobatic style. They rarely, if ever, miss their footing and fall.

Gibbons have excellent colour vision and can turn their heads and look behind them.

King of the swingers

Gibbons really know how to swing! They use their extra-long arms to speed through the canopy, reaching a top speed of 35 mph (50 kmph).

A gecko's tail acts as a rudder to direct its glide.

Gliding geckos

This small lizard has webbed feet, and flaps of skin on its sides. When it takes off, the loose skin fills with air and it gently glides down to a lower branch.

Night gliding

A sugar glider has a suitable name. It can glide on skin wings and it loves to eat the sugary sap of eucalyptus trees. A sugar glider can judge a perfect take-off and landing, even on the darkest of nights.

A twist in the tail

Some monkeys, like this spider monkey, have prehensile tails. This means they can use their tails as a fifth limb to help them to move around and pick things up – like having an extra arm.

Forest acrobats learn how to swing before they can walk!

Lianas grow from the ground up into the canopy, using a host tree for support.

Forest playground

The forest provides the perfect framework for acrobats. Woody creepers (called lianas) are useful for getting around, and canopy treetops mesh together to create "highways" between trees. To a young chimp like this one, the forest is one big, adventure playground.

Tarzan

Arghararararargh! Who can forget Tarzan's cry to his animal friends! One of the most famous stories of jungle acrobatics is the story of Tarzan – a lost baby brought up by apes. Tarzan takes his lead from his best friend, Cheetah (a chimpanzee) and swings around the forest using lianas.

Monkey mums form very close bonds with their babies.

Monkeys can look out for each other more easily in a group.

Monkey troops

Mona monkeys live in troops of up to 20 members and share friendships and family bonds. There is one ruling male in each troop, and he keeps all the females for himself. No other male gets a look in.

Apes and monkeys are human beings' nearest living relatives.

Family facts

- In some animal families mum rears the young, in some dad does it, and in others they share the burden. It varies!
- Animals often leave their families when they are adults.
- Animal brothers and sisters play together – and quarrel!

Happy families

Many rainforest animals live together in organised social groups, like our families. This is how they care for each other in the wild.

Tadpole backpack

A poison arrow frog the size of a penny piece carries her tiny tadpoles to a bromeliad pond. She deposits her load in the water and then visits the tadpoles daily until they turn into frogs.

Hitching a ride

The treetops can be dangerous for playful youngsters so many parents carry their young on their backs. In silky anteater families, it is dad that does the carrying.

Jungle giants

Elephants lumber through the jungles of Africa in family groups of up to 20. Baby elephants never stray far from their mums.

Shield bugs are very unusual. Most other insects lay their eggs and then leave them.

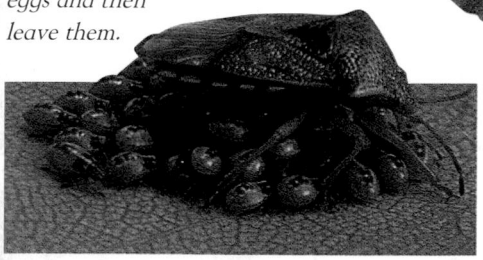

A good mother

After a female shield bug's eggs hatch, she stands guard over her bug babies. They huddle beneath her, somehow knowing that it is dangerous to venture out alone.

King of the Amazon

The jaguar is the biggest cat in the Amazon jungle. It loves meat and will eat almost any living thing. Jaguars like to prowl the riverbanks and hook out fish with their paws. They also tackle sleeping alligators. No animal is brave enough to take on a jaguar.

Jaguars are good climbers and sleep in branches.

Jaguar knights

The Aztecs were an ancient people who lived near the Amazon rainforest. They were fierce people and were always fighting their neighbours. They admired the hunting skills of the jaguar and gave the name "Jaguar knights" to the best and most fearless soldiers in their armies.

The understorey

The understorey is lit with a greenish glow, and the air is still, hot, and humid. Lazy big cats slump on branches, brightly-coloured birds whirr around flowers, and extraordinary lizards search for insect lunches.

Snakessss

Small creatures, like lizards and frogs, share the understorey with some dangerous neighbours. Snakes, such as this golden tree boa, lie in wait for passing prey.

Colourful chameleons

Not only do these unusual lizards have colourful markings, but they can also change colour. Chameleons darken to merge into their background and hide, or flash a different colour to scare away enemies.

Chameleons can look in every direction by rolling their eyes.

A hummingbird's wings beat up to 80 times per second.

The beating of their wings sounds like someone humming a tune.

Flying jewels

Hummingbirds are tiny – the smallest kind is the size of a bumblebee. They hover next to flowers, feeding on a sweet liquid inside called nectar. They lick the nectar up with long tongues that reach to the end of their spiky beaks.

A cool frog

Tree frogs need lots of water, just like pond frogs. During the day, when it is hotter, they hide in damp, leafy hollows to save water. By night, they catch insects with long, quick-action tongues.

The sticky pads on this white-lipped tree frog's toes help it grip onto wet leaves and stems.

Going batty

Love them or hate them, bats are common in the rainforest. Bats wake up at night, when the birds go home to roost, and take over their eating grounds.

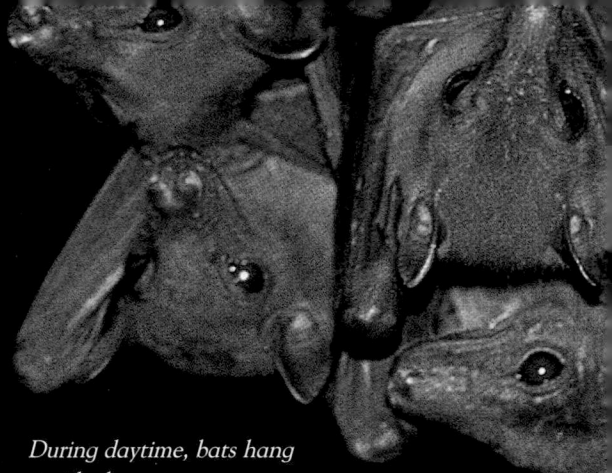

During daytime, bats hang upside down in caves or trees, sleeping and grooming themselves.

They don't mind crowds, although sometimes squabbles can break out.

Give me a pat!

This doggy-looking bat eats fruit. Also like a dog, it has an excellent sense of smell for sniffing out the juiciest fruits. It spits out seeds or passes them out in its droppings. This helps the spread of fruit trees.

Bats' wings are made of a sheet of thin skin stretched between very long fingers.

Bats are the only mammals that can fly.

Bats and flowers

This long-nosed bat loves sweet nectar, which it licks up with a long tongue from inside flowers. Its wings are hairless and as thin as paper. It wraps them around its furry body when it goes to sleep, like a blanket.

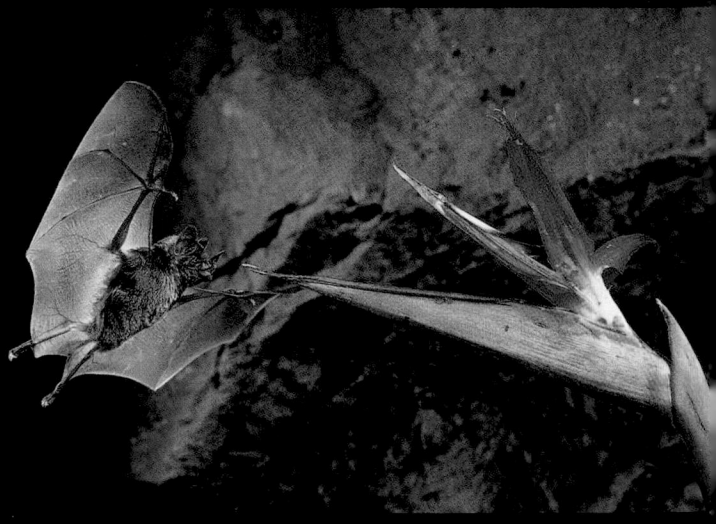

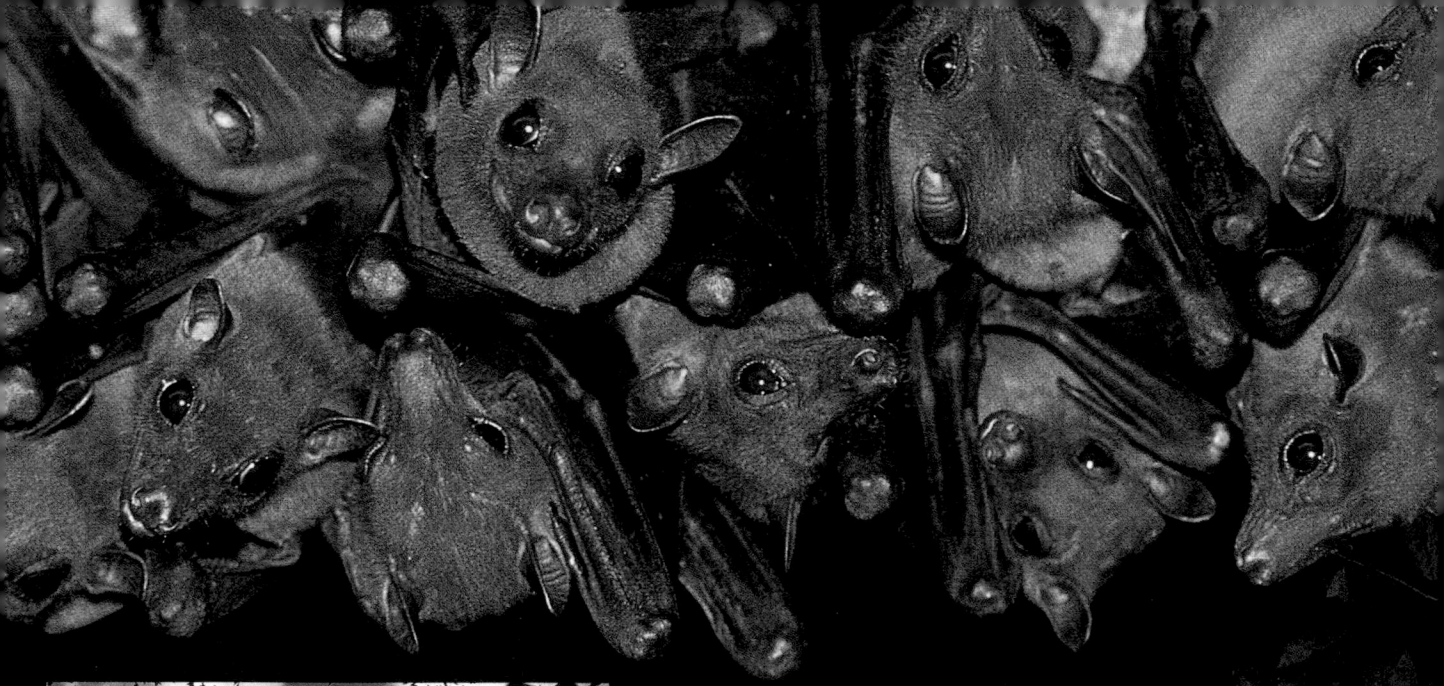

At a hidden signal, each bat takes off at the same time.

Up, up, and away!

A colony of bats wakes up at dusk. They all take off together with a great flapping of noiseless wings and set off to find food.

BATTY SIZES

The biggest bat in the world is the Malaysian flying fox. It can have a wingspan as wide as a car – 1,5 m (5 ft). The smallest bat is the bumblebee bat. It is only 3 cm (1 in) long and weighs 2 g (0.05 oz) – about the size of your big toe.

Vampire bats

This nasty little critter creeps up on sleeping animals and sinks in its fangs. The animal can't feel the bite because the bat has special spit that numbs pain. The bat then laps up blood from the wound.

They drink an egg-cupful of blood each night.

Woody words

Camouflage A disguise that makes an animal seem to merge into the background.

Imitation When animals don't look like animals at all, but resemble something their enemies would overlook or never think of eating.

Spot the bug

Can you see the insect in this picture? An insect hunter is sure to overlook this false leaf katydid as it crawls across a tree stump. It even has a hole in its head to make it look like a caterpillar has taken a nibble.

Camouflage

In the jungle, you could be surrounded by animals and not know it. Suddenly, a leaf scurries away or a tree-trunk changes shape, and you realise you're being watched...

Thorn bugs

A bird would think twice before gobbling up one of these thorny insects – that's if it knew they were insects in the first place!

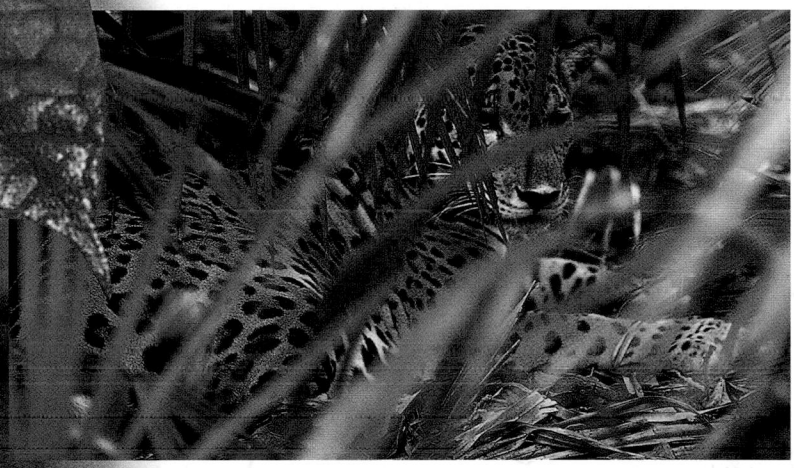

Hiding in the shadows

An unsuspecting wild pig could be standing right next to this jaguar and not notice it. The spotty markings on its coat look like the sun shining on shady leaves.

Freeze!

An iguana freezes on a tree-trunk, and, as if by magic, almost totally disappears. Its superb camouflage blends its shape into the tree-trunk. It is only when the iguana moves off that it can be seen again.

Asian leaf frog

A forest floor frog does an amazing impression of a dead leaf. Its pointed snout and hooded eyes add to the leafy effect.

The frog keeps very still and waits for prey to pass.

Lying low

Forest floor animals wind their way between trees across a carpet of dead leaves. The gloom hums with the buzz of insects, and bushes rustle as hidden predators choose their moment to pounce.

Armoured armadillos

Giant armadillos (the size of sheep) use powerful claws to dig for insects and worms. Scaly armour protects their backs from big cats as they dig.

Forest facts

- Spiders are not insects. They have eight legs making them "arachnids".
- Armadillos have 100 teeth but they hardly use them.
- Gorillas like to take it easy! They sleep for 13 hours every night and also rest for several hours at midday.

Insect armies

The jungle is alive with insects as they busily go about their daily tasks. Many live in communities that are similar to armies.

Wasp architects

Paper wasps chew up wood to make strong, light paper. They use the paper to build a cluster of cells for the queen wasp's grubs to live in. Workers collect insects and pieces of caterpillar for the grubs to eat.

Leaf-cutter ants can strip a bush of all its leaves in one night.

Tiny farmers

Leaf-cutter ants carry leaf fragments back to their underground nests. The chewed leaves make ideal compost for growing fungi – the ants' food.

Insect army ranks

Queen The only one that lays eggs. The whole insect army serves the queen.

Soldier A defender of the colony, who will fight to protect the nest from attack.

Worker A manual labourer (i.e. builder, farmer, or hunter).

Gorilla picnic

Gorillas live in family groups and work together to protect their territory and young. They sit on the forest floor, eating leaves and grunting to each other. They huff and puff, hiccup, and even burp!

Nothing wasted

Fungi grows easily on the dank, dark forest floor. The air is heavy with the smell of decay as it feeds on rotting leaves.

This stinkhorn is one of millions of fungi that eventually break down dead matter.

Hairy hunters

A curly-haired tarantula as big as a man's fist emerges from its silk-lined burrow after dark. It creeps up on prey and paralyses it with a venomous bite. The spider then sucks up the contents of its victim's body.

Ant camp

Army ants make a camp by locking themselves together with their legs and jaws. This solid mass of live ants has their queen and her eggs at the centre. When they have stripped the local area of food, the camp moves on.

On the rampage

At dawn, worker army ants and some soldier guards set off to hunt, forming a long column that snakes across the forest floor. They attack and kill anything that gets in their way, even large animals.

A soldier in defensive position

Blood-sucking mosquitoes lurk in all areas of the jungle. Only females bite, though.

Army ants are the most dangerous ants in the world.

All worker leaf-cutter ants are female. A few special males and females leave the nest to make new colonies.

Termite builders

As builders, termites are second only to people. They use strong clay to build this amazing umbrella-shaped home. Termites rarely leave their nest as they have everything they need inside.

Hunting

In the rainforest, venturing out to find food is a dangerous job – it's nothing like a trip to the supermarket! You have to be careful *and* lucky. There are traps and ambushes laid everywhere.

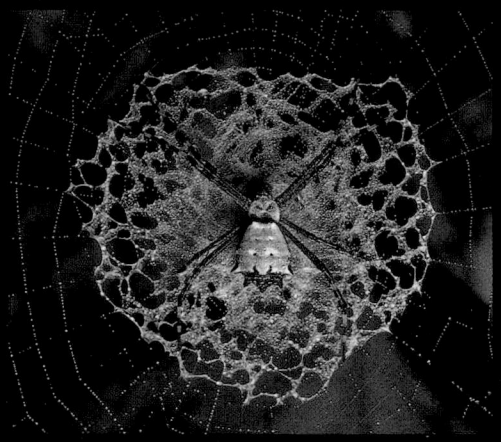

Lying in wait
There are millions of spiders in the jungle, some as big as your hand. This orb weaver spider waits for insects to fly into its sticky web.

The mantis is weighed down by its fat bottom-half, so it will not over-balance.

Its front feet have spikes to help it hold onto prey.

Good catch!
A praying mantis has launched itself towards a passing fly and caught it with its front legs. The fly had no idea it was so close to danger – the praying mantis is a master of camouflage.

Poised to strike, eyes alert...

"S" for speed
This poisonous white-lipped tree viper holds the top of its long, slithery body in an S-shape so it can strike out quickly.

Hunting for food? Watch out you're not someone else's dinner!

Pop-eye

This western tarsier looks surprised to have caught such a large moth, but it's thanks to its big eyes that it can see in the dark. Many animals hunt under the cover of night.

The snake's mouth and skin stretch to fit the whole frog into its long tummy.

Frog's legs

A forest floor snake catches a fat frog. Poison in the snake's fangs kills the frog, then the snake swallows the frog whole.

this fearsome viper lies in wait for passing prey.

Timid tapir

A tapir sticks its head out to survey the river scene. Easily startled, this timid vegetarian is an excellent swimmer and can stay underwater for many minutes if it needs to hide from a hungry jaguar.

A tapir's nose is stuck to its upper lip, making a useful trunk for tearing leaves off branches.

River trivia

- Capybaras are the biggest rodents in the world. They are the same size as pigs.
- Female anacondas are five times longer than the males. They can grow as long as 8 m (26 ft 3 in).

Jungle river water is often yellowy-brown and murky.

Riverbanks

Jungle riverbanks are alive with wildlife. Gentle plant eaters browse the thick vegetation, graceful birds show off their fishing skills, and giant snakes lie in wait for passing crocodiles...

Walking on water

This basilisk lizard can escape enemies in a surprising way. Its back feet have long toes with flaps of skin between them so it can skid across the surface of water.

Bird ballet

These elegant great white egrets patiently stalk the river, snapping up frogs and insects as well as fish. At dusk they return to their nests in the trees to roost.

Capybaras eat bankside vegetation.

Giant guinea pigs

Close relations of guinea pigs, capybaras are good swimmers thanks to their partially-webbed feet. This makes them clumsy and slow on land, however, like ducks. They live in groups of 10 to 100.

Crocodile for dinner, please!

Anacondas – the biggest snakes in the world – can be twice as long as street lamps. One of the few predators of adult crocodiles, an anaconda will squeeze a croc to death, then eat it whole.

A crocodile meal will satisfy this big snake for about a month.

Watery world

Another, entirely different group of creatures lives in jungle waterways. Many of these are gentle and harmless. Others it is wise to avoid.

Crocodile teeth can only grip and rip. Crocs can't chew or munch. They spin in the water to tear off bite-sized chunks.

Floating gardens

In some places, jungle rivers are slow-moving, shallow, and swampy. These areas are a paradise for plants. Water hyacinths (right) grow quickly, forming tangled rafts on the surface.

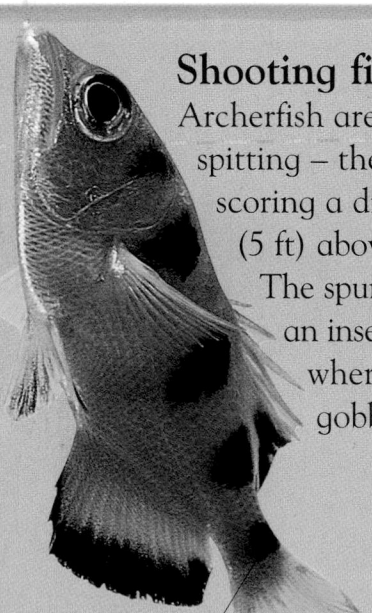

Shooting fish

Archerfish are very skilled at spitting – they are capable of scoring a direct hit 1.5 m (5 ft) above the surface. The spurt of water knocks an insect into the water where the archerfish gobbles it up.

Trailing, feathery roots absorb nutrients from the water.

These black patches look like shadows from above, so the fish can easily hide.

Amazon manatee

This slow-moving mammal browses water plants along the mighty Amazon River. It is a sociable creature and usually lives in a small group.

Manatees are often called by their nickname "sea cows".

River trivia

- Archerfish have finely adapted eyes and can see better through murky swamp water than clear water.
- Crocodiles eat about once a week.
- Not all piranhas are dangerous – only four out of 18 species will attack a human.

Death roll

A floating log seems to come to life when a caiman lunges at its prey. The struggling beast is held in the croc's jaws and turned round and round until it drowns.

Small but deadly

A school of red piranha fish can tear a large animal to pieces in minutes. They can get into such a feeding frenzy that they take bites out of each other!

Each piranha can only take a small amount of flesh in one bite. They are only successful feeders in large groups.

This is a young spectacled caiman. Caiman are a type of crocodile.

WORLD RECORD HOLDERS

Red piranhas hold the world record for being the most ferocious fish. In 1981, it was reported that piranhas attacked and ate more than 300 people when an overloaded boat sank at Obidos, Brazil. This kind of attack is not common, however!

Jaws

Although this black piranha fish is strictly vegetarian, it is armed with rows of razor-sharp teeth. Indians in the Amazon jungle use piranha jaws as scissors.

Night life

For many jungle creatures, the Sun going down is an alarm clock to get up. Animals that wake up at night are called "nocturnal" and have special features for survival in the dark.

The jungle is never completely dark. Tiny lights flicker on and off in a beautiful natural light show as fireflies meet up in bushes.

Hide and seek

A jaguarundi has large eyes which help it to see in the dark. These small cats are hard to find in the rainforest. They are excellent climbers and speed around the branches.

Jaguarundis hunt small birds, mice, and lizards that live in the trees.

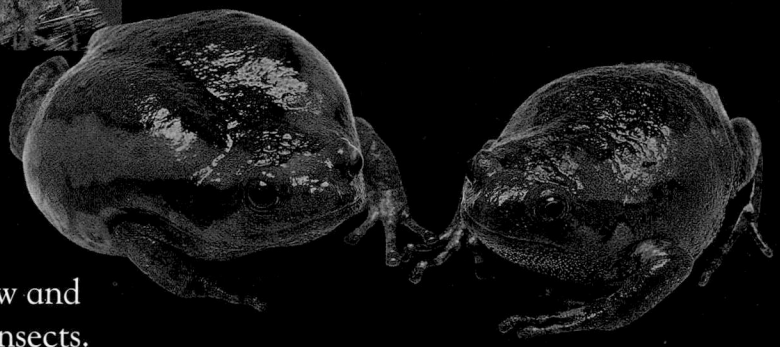

Toad in the hole

For these toads, life is safer underground or in the dark. They spend the day in a forest floor burrow and come out at night to eat insects.

Fly fishing

Fishing bats don't need to see well as they have amazing hearing. They can "hear" the size and shape of fish in the river just by sensing the ripples on the surface. They hook fish out with their claws, then kill the prey with their teeth.

Owl butterfly

The spot on this butterfly's wing fools nocturnal insect hunters. In the dark they think it is a beady owl's eye (many small animals prefer to avoid owls!) – rather than the wing of a juicy butterfly.

Butterflies have four life stages: egg, caterpillar, pupa, then butterfly. This leaf could have been eaten by an owl butterfly caterpillar.

Big cats prowl

This Indian tiger is a nocturnal hunter of forest deer and bush pigs. Its long whiskers help it feel its way around, and it can see in the dark five times better than a human being.

Forest facts

- Owl butterflies are as big as dinner plates, with wing spans up to 20 cm (8 in).
- A tiger's roar can be heard 2.5 km (1.5 miles) away – that's very noisy indeed!
- Don't pick a fight with a tiger – they have the strength of 10 men.
- Fishing bats eat while flying or hanging upside down.

Wanted: daredevil scientists!
A brave scientist risks life and limb to explore the top of a tropical rainforest tree. These areas could be home to undiscovered species of plant and animal life.

Collecting bugs
A scientist and student collect and analyse insects. Scientists believe that we have found less than half of the different types of creepy crawlies living in tropical rainforests.

Exploring the jungle

The jungle gives up its secrets slowly. After 200 years of study, we still have a lot to discover. We may yet find a cure for cancer, from a plant without a name, in a distant forest.

Amazonian Indians invented hammocks.

In harmony

Jungle people have lived in the rainforest for thousands of years. They know many of its secrets, and can teach us their unique skills and knowledge of the wildlife.

Huge chemists

Some ingredients in medicines come from jungle plants. The more we explore the rainforests, the more likely it is we will find plants that can cure the world's most serious diseases.

The seeds in this ouabain pod can help treat heart problems.

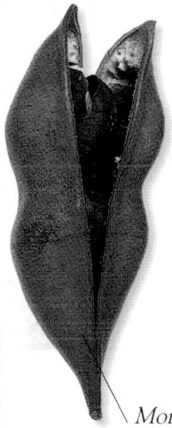

Moreton bay chestnut seeds brought hope to people with HIV.

This hard fruit treats some skin diseases.

This yam can help people with arthritis.

Rosy periwinkle plants can help treat cancer.

Protecting animals

Some rainforest animals are "endangered", which means there are not very many left in the world. These animals need extra help to survive.

Orang-utans are endangered. As a result, orang-utan sanctuaries have been set up in jungle areas where they can live undisturbed.

EARLY EXPLORERS

When early European explorers came back from their trips into the Amazon rainforest, they said they had seen men with one leg who could run like the wind, bat people who lived in holes, and beings that were half man, half fish. People outside the forest didn't know what to believe!

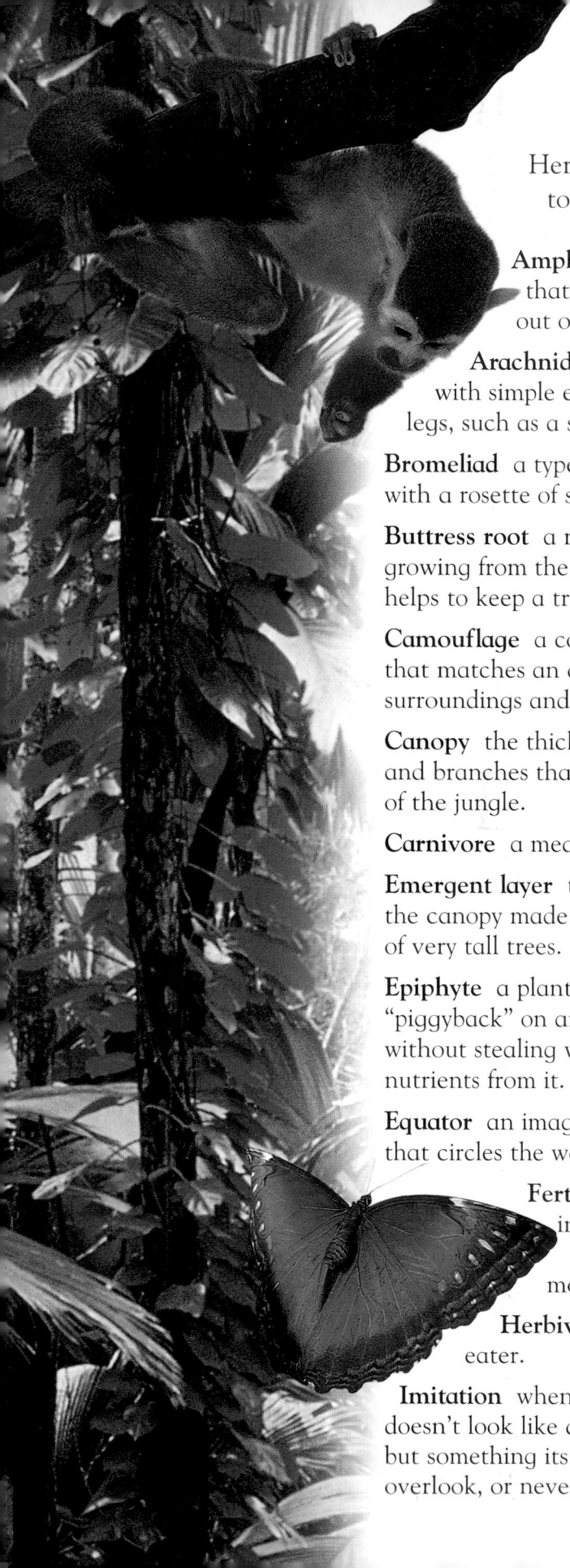

Glossary

Here are the meanings of some words it is useful to know when learning about the rainforests.

Amphibian an animal that can live in and out of water.

Arachnid an animal with simple eyes and eight legs, such as a spider.

Bromeliad a type of epiphyte with a rosette of stiff leaves.

Buttress root a root, often growing from the trunk, that helps to keep a tree upright.

Camouflage a colour or pattern that matches an animal's surroundings and helps disguise it.

Canopy the thick layer of leaves and branches that form the "roof" of the jungle.

Carnivore a meat eater.

Emergent layer the layer above the canopy made by the crowns of very tall trees.

Epiphyte a plant that grows "piggyback" on another plant, without stealing water or nutrients from it.

Equator an imaginary line that circles the world like a belt.

Fertile (soil) rich in nutrients, where plants can grow more easily.

Herbivore a plant eater.

Imitation when an animal doesn't look like an animal at all, but something its predators would overlook, or never eat.

Insect an animal with three parts to its body and six legs, such as a fly or ant.

Liana a creeping plant.

Mammal an animal that has hair and feeds its young with milk.

Nectar the sweet liquid inside flowers.

Nocturnal active at night.

Nutrients "food" that plants and animals need to grow and live healthily.

Omnivore a plant and meat eater.

Predator an animal that hunts other animals for food.

Prehensile tail a tail that can grasp (like a hand).

Prey an animal hunted for food.

Reptile an animal that has scales and lays eggs.

Rodent a mammal that has long front teeth, like guinea pigs.

Roost to rest or sleep, often in a tree.

Sapling a young tree.

Tropics the hot area that runs around the world in a band, either side of the equator.

Understorey the layer below the canopy, made up of smaller trees and bushes.

Wingspan the distance from wing-tip to wing-tip.

Animal alphabet

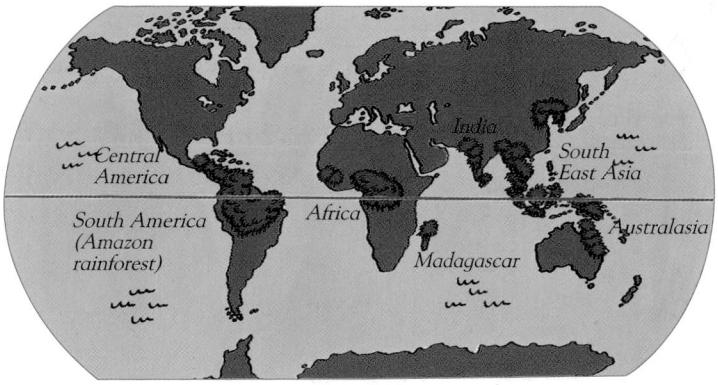

Every animal found in this book is listed here, along with its page number and which area of tropical rainforest it comes from.

Anaconda 38, 39
South America

Ants (in ant plant) 18
South East Asia

Archer fish 40
South East Asia, Australia

Army ants 35
Central and South America

Asian leaf frog 31
South East Asia

Basalisk lizard 39
Central and South America

Blue morpho butterfly 14
Central and South America

Capybara 38, 39
South America

Chameleon 27
Madagascar

Chimpanzee 23
Africa

Colobus monkey (Black and white) 15
Africa

Colugo 14, 19
South East Asia

Common marmoset 14
Central and South America

Crocodile (Spectacled caiman) 7, 9, 41
Central and South America

Elephant (African) 25
Africa (Asian elephants live in Indian jungles)

Emperor tamarin 8, 9
South America

False leaf katydid 30
Central and South America

Fishing bat 42, 43
Central and South America

Fruit bat 28
All

Gecko (flying) 22-23
South East Asia

Giant armadillo 32
South America

Gibbon (Siamang) 22
South East Asia

Golden tree boa 27
Central and South America

Gorilla 5, 32, 33
Africa

Great white egret 39
All

Green tree python 20-21
Australasia

Hermit hummingbird 18
Central and South America

Hummingbird (Violet-eared) 27
Central and South America

Iguana (Green) 9, 21, 31
Central and South America

Jaguar 26, 31
South America

Jaguarundi 42
South America

King vulture 17
Central and South America

Leaf-cutter ants 34-35
Central and South America

Long-nosed bat 28
South America

Macaw 16
Central and South America

Manatee (Amazon) 40
South America

Mona monkey 24
Africa

Mosquitos 35
All

Orang-utan 19, 45
South East Asia

Orb weaver spider 36
All

Owl butterfly 43
Central and South America

Paper wasps 34
Central America

Parakeet (Yellow-chevroned) 17
Central and South America

Philippine eagle 17
Only found in the Philippines (South East Asia)

Piranha fish 7, 40-41
South America

Poison arrow frog 9, 25
Central and South America

Postman butterfly 8
Central and South America

Praying mantis 36
All

Rainbow lorikeet 16-17
Australasia

Red-eyed tree frog 5
Central America

Shield bug 25
South East Asia

Silky anteater 25
Central and South America

Sloth 20
Central and South America

Spider monkey 23
Central and South America

Squirrel monkey 21
Central and South America

Sugar glider 22
Australasia

Tapir (Brazilian) 38
South America

Tarantula (Curly-haired) 33
Central and South America

Termites 35
All

Thorn bug 31
Central and South America

Tiger (Indian) 43
India

Toad (Asian burrowing) 42
South East Asia

Toucan 8, 9
Central and South America

Tree kangaroo 15
Australasia

Vampire bat 29
Central and South America

Western tarsier 37
South East Asia

White-lipped tree frog 27
South East Asia and Australasia

White-lipped tree viper 36-37
South East Asia

Index

Amazon rainforest, 8, 13, 14, 26
Amazon River, 40
Amazonian Indian, 41, 45
amphibian, 9
Aztecs, 26

bats, 28-29, 42
birds, 8, 16-17
bromeliad, 11, 18
butterfly, 8, 9, 14, 43
buttress root, 10

camouflage, 30-31
canopy, 6, 7, 21
carnivore, 9
caterpillar, 20, 43
clearing, 10
creeper, 12

disease, medicine for, 45

emergent layer, 6, 10, 14
endangered animals, 45
epiphyte, 11, 12, 21
equator, 5
exploring, 44-45

flowers, 12-13, 21
food, hunting, 36-37
forest floor, 7, 32-33
frogs, 7, 9, 18, 27, 37
fungi, 33

gliding, 22

hammock, 45
heliconia, 12
herbivore, 9
hunting, 36-37

Indian, Amazonian, 41, 45

insects, 8, 9, 34-35, 44

leaves, 21
liana, 12, 23
lobster claw, 12

mammal, 8
medicine, 4, 45
monkeys, 6, 21

nectar, 12, 28
nests, 18-19
nocturnal animals, 42-43
nutrients, 11
nuts, 16

omnivore, 9
orchid, 12

parasite, 12
parrots, 6, 16, 17
pitcher plant, 12

rafflesia, 12
rain, 5
reptile, 9, 21
rivers, 5, 7, 38-39, 40-41
roots, 10, 11
rubber, 13

sapling, 10, 11
scientist, 44-45
snakes, 9, 27, 36-37
soil, 8, 11
spiders, 32, 36
stinkhorn, 33

tail, prehensile, 23
Tarzan, 23
temperature, 5
toads, 9, 42
trees, 6-7, 10-11
troop, monkey, 24
tropical rainforests, 5

understorey, 7, 26-27

vines, 12

water hyacinth, 40
weather, 5
wings, 14, 22, 28

Rainbow lorikeet

Useful websites

Animals of the Rainforest *Jungle animals with bite-sized information and great colour pictures.*
www.animalsoftherainforest.com

Toucan Sam's Encyclopedia of the Rainforest *Everything you need to know, with Toucan Sam as your guide.*
www.toucansam.kelloggs.ca/eng/enter.htm

Zoom Rainforests *It's all here. Colour-in animal printouts.*
www.EnchantedLearning.com/subjects/rainforest

Rainforest Action Network *Lot of info (and good jungle sound effects), as well as ways to help preserve the rainforests.*
www.ran.org/kids_action/index1.html

Virtual Rainforest *Find out what's hiding behind the leaves.*
www.msu.edu/~urquhar5/tour/active.html

Acknowledgements

Dorling Kindersley would like to thank:
Hilary Bird for preparing the index; Emily Bolam for original artwork; additional picture researchers, Bridget Tily and Sean Hunter; and Simon Holland for editorial assistance.

Picture credits

The publisher would like to thank the following for their kind permission to reproduce their photographs:
a=above; c=centre; b=below; l=left; r=right; t=top;

Ardea London Ltd: Kenneth W. Fink 17cr; **Bruce Coleman Ltd:** 26c, 27bl, 29cl, 29t; Bruce Coleman Inc 12c; Alain Compost 19br; Gerald S. Cubitt 12bl; M.P.L.Fogden 25cr(a); Steven C Kaufman 12cl; Joe McDonald 39tr; Luiz Claudio Marigo 8cr(a), 11br; Rod Williams 17cb; **Robert Harding Picture Library:** 10b, 10t; Frans Lantin/Minden Pictures 23tl; Minden Pictures 33tl; **Chris Mattison:** 36bc; Chris Mattison 30c, 31r; **Minden Pictures:** Mark Moffett 44c; **N.H.P.A.:** 22bl, 28br, 36tr, 42c, 42bc, 43c; G.I. Bernard 31cl; James Carmichael JR 5cl; Planet Earth/Gary Bell 32l; Kevin Schafer 33cr; Martin Wendler 39bl;**Oxford Scientific Films:** 37c; John Brown 39cr; Joe Macdonald 18bl; Partridge Films Ltd 25cl; Philip Sharpe 36tl; P. & W. Ward 14cr; **Planet Earth Pictures:** 27r; Andre Bartschi 16c, 17r; Beth Davidow 9c; Ken Lucas 14c; Florian Mollers 10c; Jonathan P. Scott 15cl; **Plant Pictures World Wide:** 26 background; **Raleigh International Picture Library:** Paul Claxton 44cr(b); **Science Photo Library:** Fletcher & Baylis 13c; Tom McHugh 22l; **Still Pictures:** Andre Bartschi/Still Pictures 5cr; Compost/Visage/Still Pictures 19c; Mark Edwards 40br; Klein/Hubert 15tr; **getty images stone:** Art Wolfe 3r; **Telegraph Colour Library:** J.P. Nacivet 46l; 47r; Planet Earth/Andre Bartschi 31cr(b); Gail Shumway 1c; **Gunter Ziesler:** 18tr; Gunter Ziesler 23r, 32cr(b), 38c, 39cl.

Jacket: **Bruce Coleman Ltd:** Alain Compost br; **Images Colour Library:** c.